THOUGHTS, HOPES, OPINIONS, AND DREAMS

THOUGHTS, HOPES, OPINIONS, AND DREAMS

POETIC DIARY OF A SCHIZOPHRENIC

by

ATIF ZAIN MIRZA

authorHOUSE®

AuthorHouse™ UK
1663 Liberty Drive
Bloomington, IN 47403 USA
www.authorhouse.co.uk
Phone: 0800.197.4150

Published by AuthorHouse 03/19/2015

ISBN: 978-1-4678-9665-8 (sc)
ISBN: 978-1-4678-9664-1 (e)

Contents

Dedication to Family

Sorry for the things I will put you through
Sorry for the things I feel I have to do

Sorry for all the upcoming tough days and nights
Sorry for the thing you may consider as not being right

Sorry for the things I am going to say
Sorry for the stress on you through the ins and outs of your day

Sorry for the stress and strain I will cause you
sorry for making you feel sad and blue

I hope you all can forgive me for what I will put you through
I hope this will help you understand why I did it and why I behave the
way I do

To my family, sorry

Dedication to friends

I have got some special friends that have impacted my life
helping me to see that one day things could be alright

They gave me strength in moments where I was in need
helping with my emotions to plant and nurture some very important seeds

They help me to realise that goodness isn't something that is far away from me
with all I have to do is work hard and be willing to believe

I had to be open to the possibility of good things being able to be true
holding on to the rope of Allah the Compassionate when it comes to the things that I do

They are always there when I need and they always lend an ear
they help me realise that change was always near

Now thanks to these friends I am able to have people around
these friends don't add to my sorrow but help me when I am feeling down

To my Special friends of the Jinn

May Allah who is the only needed guide and supporter
do for them as he has permitted that they do for me

Ameen

The Opening part 1

This book is about how I deal with the hardships that have come to see
also how I move forward and find space to breathe

How I face challenging circumstances that have appeared in my life
how I find strength and what makes me think that everything will one
day be alright

My thoughts, hopes, opinion and dreams
the things I get told and some things I have seen

These are the things I have come to believe are true
all I am doing is sharing them with people like you

Maybe you'll find them interesting,
maybe you'll laugh

maybe you'll start to consider what voice hearing is all about
as a 'voice hearer' one thing I'll say life has changed in some interesting
ways

These are my intimate thoughts I am allowing you to see
I hope you reflect on what's affecting me

By Atif Zain Mirza

The Opening part 2

I'm classified as a voice hearer
wait till you read about some of the things that are happening to me

Everything I have written here is true
when you come to know some of the types of things that I go through

If you were in my shoes what would you choose to be the truth?

My life might be strange to hear about
I'd like to tell you something and that's lies are not here

I know it's a bit unbelievable but what can I do?
I feel obligated to tell my story to people like you

Some might seem really nice but for me to experience it's a real struggle
Some might seem strange and bizarre and leave you in a puzzle

I have had to learn patients and at times and with my emotions to juggle
I got attacked by Jinns and I'm left in a muddle

all I do is endure this reality of mine
to be quite honest it is the only reason why I am healing and beginning
to feel fine

I suppose it's the way it's written for someone like me
it's even at times a little hard to believe

I can't deny what I have come to see
it's only my understanding that changes and hopefully that you will see

This isn't a joke
these are the things which I experience on the inside
I really want you to think about the things which I will come to describe

In my life I have been through a lot. As a child I had so called relationships as some might say but to me, I was mis-used. People in my life had their way with me and then when they were finished they left me alone. On top of that I confided in so called friends and they let me down by telling the brother of one of my 'partners' and he tried to do an honor killing but instead of killing me himself he sent Jinn devils after me to torture me and kill me. In the beginning I didn't understand what was going on but soon I figured it out.

Now I'm left with picking up the pieces of my life after almost ending it in 2 failed attempts at suicide and I'm sharing the lessons I've learnt hoping someone can find them useful in overcoming depression as I did with the key element, support.

Filled with Hate

I have suffered a lot of trauma
With the things I've been through
It caused me to do things
Which were un-natural for me to do

I've experienced things
Which I hate to remember
I've had nobody to turn to
when I needed help in 2014's December

My feelings go to extremes
I find it difficult to cope
Positivity is difficult to embrace
And I am unable to hold on to hope

I find hating myself easier
when it comes to having an opinion about who I am
Finding myself thinking what's in store
and thinking what plan does Allah (swt) for me have

I find it easier to believe
Love for me shouldn't become true
But Jinn's constantly bombard me saying
yes, even for you

It's not very easy
to consider such words
could I really be someone
who Love he deserves?

Full of worry

What do I do?
What do I believe?
I have experienced some things that most people can't even conceive

My life is full of difficulties that cause me stress and pain
They challenge my perception of reality which makes happiness difficult
to maintain

I am becoming scared of my future
Again, I am scared of what could one day come to be
I'm scared of what could happen
Again, I'm scared of the things I could come to see

With no person to turn to
I need to find a way to be strong
I need to find a way to stand firm
I need to find something to help me go on

My journey is so complicated
The twist and turns cause me to struggle with life's daily events
I need an explanation that satisfies me
Not one that causes me to live in suspense

Suicide

I've been contemplating suicide
hoping it could be
A sweet release for someone
the right direction for me

I'm thinking It's an avenue
I should wilingly explore
searching for the instance
where I can be no more

I'm thinking it should be something
I should endure
My life is always going to be difficult
with me feeling I don't want to take anymore

I'm hoping it will be something
to bring me much needed relief
I have an unforgiving enemy
who will be happy if in life I don't compete

I don't know what to do
with all the pain I see in store
It's difficult, unsettling
all I see coming my way is more

More pain, more sorrow
more difficulties coming my way
It happens all the time
Again, it happens everyday

I endure torture so extreme
Magic at the hand of my kin
he makes use of Jinn's
to have his way and many battles he tends to win

I want to get away from them
about me they do not care
It's something I have to live with
It's something I have to bear

That's why I thought suicide
It could be something for me
that could be my solution
It could be something that happiness it could bring

Jumble

This world is a jumble
I feel like I'm prey
Learning to doing Jihad
As I go through my day

It's hard to get things right
I know life's a journey
Things are getting tough
I'm not seeing so clearly

What do I do with what I see on display?
Shall I walk away or learn how to play?

Intense emotions

Do you know what it's like to have emotions beyond all you know how
to share?
Maddening, debilitating beyond compare

Obsessive and Impulsive
Not plain to see
Not to my family
Not to anybody

It's driving me mad
It's making me crazy
It's so intense
It's making me lazy

To bathe to shave
Or even to wash
I feel it so much
It's making time stop

What can I do?
How do I get through?
I am in need of discipline
When it comes to the things I pursue.

Annoyance

I'm tired of hearing that I am not really ill
by those same old people who are wanting me to be still and chill

They seem to think I just mess about and I only take a pill
they don't know what I go through and what ALLAH the ALMIGHTY
has willed

I wish they could know what I really go through
it has me thinking about what they would do

If they only knew what I go through
then they'd understand and then they'd have a clue

It's not very easy for me every day is a challenge
so that they know I only just manage

Life is not easy and it get's hard to see
which is the best way to turn because the path is not very clear to me

Life is a test and you know and mine is very hard
the way I reacted it has left me severely scared

I'm not complaining though it's the way that was written for me
I'm still on my journey to see what I can be

It's not going be easy and I guess my life not meant to be so
I'm still struggling and striving to see what direction I decide to go

Life is a journey and journeys can be rough
there are times when I need to be patient especially when it gets really
tough

It's very true, you earn everything that your given
now let's see if I can keep up with my life's irregular rhythm

Self-destruction

Do you know what it's like to want to destroy yourself because I couldn't
bear to see Memories of encounters I couldn't believe which I'd allowed
to enter my life and be

They unsettled me in way's destroying things inside
so to protect myself I'd attempted to make myself numb and blind.

I wish you could have faced it, moved forward and got better
the pain was unbearable and I didn't know how to bear the stormy
weather

Enjoying life in the same way again is hard because my heart is damaged
when I use it in a normal way it's hard to manage

This fact is hard and makes certain situations difficult to take
it has me feeling that at certain points I'm going to break

I hope to gain strength that stops me from feeling blue
which stops me from doing what should be natural to do

I keep away from affection because it's hard to take
I've got friends in place to help when I get in that state

They give me the things needed that help which gives strength to cope
bringing me closer to ease but I'm on a slippery slope

Addiction

Have you ever had an addiction because you could bear to see
what happened around you and what facts had come to be?

Have you ever had an addiction because you couldn't let things go?
Were events hard to take?
Did everything moving in slow mo?

Have you ever had an addiction because you mood wouldn't keep?
Did it make what was going on around you something you couldn't
stand to see?

Like can become hard
With situations becoming difficult to deal with
We need some help and support
When it come to our ability to get by and live

The Supportive

They can see my emotions and they won't pass them by,
they have paid such attention that they see clearly what I have going on inside

They don't take advantage by letting me commit major crimes
instead they get in the way of it as if they can see something in my eyes

I'm being restrained from making mistakes of that kind of degree
they don't get in the way if that's the way I need it to be

They want me to behave and do good things and good stuff
while getting in the way especially when I'm feeling really rough

They seem to really care about what I go through
helping when things get to difficult with me losing sight on what I want to do

They don't just give me the right answer
they help me get to a place where I can decide

they always get me to consider
the feelings that I have inside

Whatever I do they support me until my perception begins to clear
, they help me get to a place where a free and informed decision is near

It's like they are family and they are here to help
they seem to really care about me even when I'm unable to do so myself

Strengthen Foundations

They want to strengthen my foundations
and destroy all falsehoods I hide

they don't let my feelings pass by
regardless of what I say and how much it hurts inside

They want me to believe
love for me can be true

they will stick to me
even if they have to use glue

They are trying to give me hope
letting me know that I should be patient and endure

if I want them to stop
I have to sincerely say is no more

I don't know what to do at times the pain can seem much to manage
they seem to suggest that I should sit back and try my best to manage

Strengthen Sincerity

They seem to be strengthening my sincerity
so that I don't easily tell lies

they want me to feel my emotions and to embrace them
getting to know what I have going on inside

This is hard for me to do I want to run away from these feeling
the place they want me to get to I keep saying `you must be dreaming'

All they do is guide me they don't force me into stuff
they don't give me the answer but sometimes they give me a little push

Facing these feelings that I have is hard, it is a great ordeal
my heart is full of worry, it's difficult to do and all I want to do is conceal

This makes life difficult
I don't know whether to stay or get away

They are so precise in their dealings with me
I don't know if I want to do what they say

Strengthen Emotions

They want to strengthen my emotions they won't let me build on a lie
regardless of what I say and from what I want to hide

They want me to face the reality of the positions I hold
they won't let me conceal what I feel or even let certain things go

But when I am in distress they know I need a rest
if I act out in pain they don't judge they pick up the mess

This cycle really helps it is a comfort to know
regardless of how I react, it's only love, respect, compassion, mercy and
understanding that will be shown

Encouragement

They want me to be confident
they don't want me to be small and hide

they want me to be strong
and have all that in my eyes

They want me to stand up tall and for me to believe
that I am capable even if it's hard for me to conceive

They don't want me to deny the person I have come to be
whilst telling me that they want me to see

I am respected even if it is hard for me to believe
they'll stand by me and help me to cope and find ease

Sometimes it seems like it's too good to be true
they seem to keep encourage me while assisting me with the things I go
through

Distance needed

Affection is a difficult emotion
They must let it pass by
Regardless of the effects
It will have on the insides

They must see that for me
This can be difficult to see
Even though they have been told
Of the way it's meant for me

I need to keep away
The pain is too much to bear
They should be able to see how much
From what they see in my stare

I wish they would stop reminding me,
Of what the possibilities could be,
I wish they would keep away
Because it's difficult for me to see

Troubled by beauty

I'm seeing women's beauty
It overwhelms, I want to get away,
It get's so overwhelming
Seeing it all parts of the day

It can be so loud and inviting,
Calling me to take a peak,
I need to keep away from such things
It's even affecting my speech

My heart feels strained
It's difficult to get away,
What I need to do to keep that kind of beauty away?

On the inside I feel
Pain with what they put on display
I have to stick with patients
Waiting for comfort to come my way,

I'll do the best I can
Trying not to frown
Holding on is going to be tough

I see it's going to be an ordeal
It disrupts my flow
Highlighting how I feel

Complicated

None of my emotions are wasted
it's impossible to slip them by

they keep responding to them
like they can sense how I feel inside

They want me to accept that it is the way I really feel
also teaching me that it's wrong to deny something so real

They want me to be comfortable with how I feel inside
while softly suggest that everything will be alright

The kindness seems sincere it's hard to put up a fight
I don't know what to do it's difficult to accept and comply

Friend needed

All I see is my own truth
It can be difficult to see
What is also going on in the world, and how certain facts came to be

Things are getting really bad
And it's becoming plainer to see
Things are going to get bad like the stories on TV

Things are getting worse
And for me hope is getting further away
I want to know how to catch it needing it to cope with what society so
freely displays

I am in need of some support to help get me through
I need a friend for defence against my deepening sadness and someone
to help me with the things I need to do

Affection

This emotion is difficult they must let it pass by
regardless of the effects it will have on the insides

They must see that it is hard for me to see
regardless of what they have been told or what they have come to believe

This is difficult and let my situation be
allow me to live without this implication and let me live with ease

I wish they would give up
I wish they would let it pass by

I wish they would stop reacting to what they seem to see in my eyes

Adjust

Love is a difficult emotion,
I don't know how to reciprocate
They keep on attempting to relieve my difficulties
So that I do appreciate

It's hard to get things right
The concept is new to me
Thoughts get very troubling
I don't know how to move past the sensations that have now come to be

I wonder what it would take
To help me get through,
I wonder what to do,
With them sticking to me as if by using glue

I'm on one of life's interesting journeys
That everyone must partake
But as any, it can have difficulties
I must adjust and not misplace hope and break

My Helpers

I have a group sent to help me with the problems I go through
when I don't know how to feel or I don't know what to do

They don't make any suggestions
all they do is highlight my ideas

all I do is stumble around them
I have some things that I have come to fear

I get in a state of confusion when my options are too near
they help me choose, they guide me, to a place where things are more
clear

The difficulties that I have lie in the future that I see
the future that stands before me and the one that is available for me to
achieve

If only I felt comfortable with the person I have come to be
maybe then I would be more accepting with the choices in front of me

Hate Myself

I'm not allowed to hate myself
I can't be that type of guy

I have to look in the mirror
with a look of respect in my eyes

I have to be strong and hold on when things get tough
not being shaken when memories get that little bit rough

I have to hold on to the fact that mistakes can easily come to be
need to learn from them to make life pleasurable again for me

This can be hard, some facts are difficult to take
I'm being told that I should stand firm every time every time I get in that state

My Protectors

They don't want me to get attached to them and they make that point
very clear
when I see them they don't want me to be in a state where I would be
full of fear

They want me to be open to relationships and all the positive aspects
that they entail
wanting me to behave in a way that for me is appropriate and real

They don't want me to give up on it or just jump into it without giving it
a second thought they don't want me rushing into it without thinking in
the way that I aught

They want me to be cautious of every decision that I make
they want me to be of such quality that I won't again misplace hope and
come close to break

All they ask of me is that I am sincere and stick to what I know is true
if I do this they support me and in everything good that I do

They seem to have faith in me and give me a lot of respect
all of this can sometimes seem overwhelming but my heart
they seem to want to cleanse and protect

Imposter

I am seeing an imposter
Trying to imply
That I should be good
They have a forceful look in their eyes,

They try to look nice,
As if they are trying to help
But they don't understand the game
And that is for me to do it for myself

All they can do is remind me
Of the decisions that I have already made
So that I consider the impact of my actions and think
Do I want it that way?

These devils try to force me
So that I fall in line and behave
And have a really powerful look in their eyes
And have emptiness standing out from their gaze,

They are like bullies from when I was younger,
Getting you to do stuff
And If you don't all they do is push push push

If they were good
They would try to show me the error of my ways
Using honesty and sincerity
So that their points could be clearly made

That's way when I saw them
I though imposter
I have to do something
So I scream within
"Don't let them stop you"

Being Guided

I'm not allowed to do lip service I have to mean what I say
depending on the situation in which my point has to be made

I have to be sincere and precise in all that I do
it has to incorporate what I know and I must think of all that I can do

I am being encouraged not to misguide but reminded that mistakes can
be made
the way I react must have humility even when it comes to my gaze

It's not that I have to be perfect but I have to be the best that I can be
I must learn to be strong and do what's best including those around me

This is the path that I see, being lay down in front of me
it's hard to deny but I'm being guided in ways that are hard for me to
conceive

In a state of wonder

Have you ever felt such energy hit you it made you sit up at attention?
Have you ever felt such energy hit you and it was filled with nothing
but different kinds of affection?

Have you ever been shocked because you didn't know how to react?
Have you ever got to a point where you thought tit for tat?

Have you ever remembered something so profound it left you amazed?
Have you ever seen something so beautiful you felt like you were lost
in that very first gaze?

Have you ever wondered if, in your dreams you got shown glimpses of
your future?
Have you ever wondered why you were shown it and what it would
teach you?

Have you ever wondered what it could all mean?
Have you ever thought why you got shown it and what exactly it is you
have seen?

What can I do with what I have seen?
Should I take a chance and consider what others could only dream?

Shown Affection

What do you do with those who show you affection and they don't ask for anything in return?
They only imply that it is only something that I have the right to experience because it's something I have earned

They come at me in such a way they strike when I don't expect
it comes at me in such a way it is nothing but warm and direct

It lingers in my heart making me content and filling me with joy
it's the kind of experience that makes me feel loved and that I am a cared for special boy

They don't want me to reciprocate, they say it's only something that I must learn to accept
I am sincerely loved and the way it makes me feel they don't want me ever to reject

Reset Emotions

They are trying to bring me back to normality
But it's hard to comply,
They say it's the way I need to be
So that I can live life again and comfortably get by

It's a difficult process
I'm buried so deep inside
I have moved so very far away from the norm
They say I should do my best to comply

I have to stay the course
Trying not to hurry,
I have to let the emotions flow
Trying not to worry

I guess this is what it feels like
When one begins to heal,
Thoughts and feeling get quite uncomfortable
With things seeming too real

I have to struggle and strive
If I want to get through;
I have to hold onto truth
When it comes to everything that I do

Confidence is needed
To stick to what I feel is true
It's hard to do this
I'm unsure and still looking for what to do

Difficult Emotions

I'm feeling emotions that I have never felt before
it's unsettling and making me go down a road that makes me feel scared
and I don't think I can take much more

It's really uncomfortable I need something in place to protect
defend me from the feeling that I don't know if I can accept

I'm frozen is a state that is hard for me to define
 I need support to face the feelings and someone to help give me courage
to take it one step at a time

I suppose I need to be strong walking the path that I must partake
I need to be confidant and not get upset if I start to shake

This is a difficult journey and I feel all alone
I need support and guidance and someone to help me stay in control

Afraid to Love

I'm afraid to love
I'm afraid of being hurt
I'm afraid of being vulnerable and of the things that I could
come to learn

I'm afraid of being open
I'm afraid to let anybody in
I'm afraid of accepting someone and all that it could bring

I'm afraid to need someone
I'm afraid she won't need to back
I'm afraid I won't know what to do with her and I won't know how to
behave or how to react

I'm afraid of the pain I could cause her
I'm afraid that I won't be good enough
I'm afraid that I'm not the type of person who is easily understood

I need someone who will support me
I need someone to teach me how to act
I need someone who will nurture my feelings at those moments where I
don't know how to act

Healing Process

They are rebuilding my emotions
Helping me stay the course
It's not what I expect
Or anything I have proposed

They are helping me heal
So I can experience things that are real
I am confused and conflicted
But it has an interesting appeal

I'm not sure where it's going to go
Or when they are going to appear
I'm waiting patiently
What they are doing is elevating some of my fears

My heart feels more whole
I'm starting to feel calmer
I don't feel like I used to
Which was to sound a silent alarm

The sensation seems good
I think I'm beginning to find
Ease and comfort
In things that I can't really define

Kept on track

They know just how to entice me
They know just how to make me forget
They know the things that are needed
To keep me in check

They know what is needed
To keep me on this journey,
They know what is needed and get me to hold on
They know what to do it like I'm meant to be strong

They know the things what would attract me,
They're not letting me just be
They want me to follow their example
And they keep throwing affect up against me

They do it even if I don't want it,
They do it even if I'm mad
They do it even when if I am self destructive
They do what they can to get in the way when I'm feeling sad

It's a funny set of circumstances with all that above
I think they do it all because they are trying to show me what it's like to
really be loved.

The Supportive Part 2

They want me to get used to what it feels like to be sincerely loved
all they want is for me to accept this fact and it seems that is enough

They don't want me to feel obligated to do anything major in return
they say it's only something I have a right to experience so that I get
used to it and learn

They say it's something everybody is deserving of and for me I get it in
this special way
I get it every time I feel hurt and lonely with it happens each and every
part of the day

It's like not of my emotions are wasted and they want me to get used to
what those feelings mean to me
they are always with me so they can spring into action every time these
emotions come to be

It is a strange experience to have Jinn's behave in this way showing how
deeply they have come to care
they are so precise in the way that they show me it's like they have
always been there

I don't know what to do with all the attention it's like I'm never going to
be alone again
they are always there to support me with the feeling of acceptance which
they seem to be wanting maintained

It's like they want what's best for me and comfort is what they want me
to gain
it's like, they are always there when it is cloudy and spring into action
when there's signs it's going to rain

To be cared for by Jinn's believe me at times it's a little hard to take
I guess they don't want me ever getting to a point where I would again,
misplace hope and break

Encouraged to accept love

They use a familiar form to develop the way that things feel
doing so to cushion the blow otherwise for me it would be too real

They want me to accept their affection from deep in my inner core
always restraining what they display when I feel I can't take any more

When I think about it sincerely, it makes me nervous and I tend to shake
it's like I'm really scared of those feelings and sometimes I feel like I'm
going to break

I'm not used to feeling that way about females or thinking that women
like me in that way
I'm not used to seeing it or hearing it so plainly every time I feel that way

It can seem really overwhelming, but it seems so innocent and pure
sometimes it can make me very uncomfortable and it can have me
heading to the door

They can tell what it is I am feeling and they seem to adjust at those
points where I'm about to break
they know when I'm going to get overwhelmed so, they restrain what
they display and let me absorb only what I can take

They seem to know what they are doing like they want me to accept that
this is my fate while attempting to make things so that love for me is a
natural state

Supported

Special women seem to support, encourage and aid me and care deeply
about the things that I hear and see
they be sweet and show me affection whenever I feel low about the
person I have come to be

What they display seem to be done with sincerity never giving me what
I want or expect
What they give me far exceeds my expectations and is always warm and
comes at me direct

It's a message that penetrates my heart deep to its inner core
at times I doubt it's real but then comes so much more

They don't want me to get attached to them
they show me things that seem so innocent and pure,

They seem to be concerned about me
and are always there to reassure

It's overwhelming to see how they respond to me
there's a message that they want to come in clear,

They are friends and they will always be around me
wanting pain as something that doesn't harm when it comes near

Duty

None of my emotions are wasted
They can sense how I feel inside
They keep responding to them
Showing me things from which I want to hide

They say they do it out of duty
They say in what they are doing I should trust
They say they are doing what is needed
Touching my heart is a must

They are very consistent
Never giving me what I want or expect
From what they say they are fulfilling their duty
They don't mess around and they are very direct

They are very creative
With what they put on display
Apparently it is what is needed
And from what I see they are here to stay

It's a very difficult to experience
Seeing the things that I do
I wish they would stop doing it
And implying it is nothing but the truth

What am I suppose to do?
What am I suppose to believe?
I can't reject what they imply
About what they say is meant for me

I guess it's just something unavoidable
Something that is just my fate
It's not very easy
To accept what they are putting on my plate

Hating the way things feel

I hate the way they annoy me
I hate the way they can make me feel
I hate what they show me
Defining for me what is real

I hate the way they look at me
I hate what they are trying to portray
I hate what they are trying to make me feel
Making me feel it all parts of the day

I hate that they won't leave me alone
I hate that they are always there
I hate the fact that they are showing me things
Trying to make me care

I hate that they are so persistent
I hate that they can see what I feel inside
I hate that I can't slip anything past them
I hate that I am not able to conceal what I feel or hide

I hate that I am not able to tell them what I feel I want to say
I hate that I am not able to put the feelings I want on display
I hate that I am so weak and not able to do what I want
I hate that they seem to believe that all I am doing is putting on a front

I hate the fact that they consider everything that I say
I hate the fact that when it comes down to it I tend to agree with what
they direct my way
I hate that they may be right in all that they do
I hate the fact that I know this battle I am going to loose

I hate that they are able to persuade me
I hate that they can keep me in check
I hate that they seem to like me
I hate that my future they seem to want to protect

I don't know what to do
I want to push all that they say away
My only option is to be patient
And see what options my Creator brings my way

Complex situation

None of my emotions are wasted
It's impossible to slip them by
There's a certain way they act around them
Effecting how I feel inside

Certain things are being put on display
There are certain things that I hear
When I think of my future
I'm worried and start filling with fear

They imply a certain notion
That is difficult for me to bear
I think I am doomed
I can sense something in the air

It's not a simple situation
I am not able to sincerely object to what they say
My heart is inclined to like it
It can be difficult for me to feel that way

I wonder what is needed
To put what I want on display
I wonder what I can do
To stop me feeling this way

I wonder what it would take
To help me get through
I'm saddened because deep down I know
The direction they want me to go is difficult for me to choose

Strange surroundings

I seem to have a special creation
Who have chosen to come to my aid
They have the skills needed
So I always listen to what they say

They also have the skills needed
To see through my attempts to put what I want on display
Supposedly they are doing what they need
So honesty and sincerity is maintained

Apparently they have to reconnect me
With how I really feel inside
They have to do what is needed
To make sure 'truth' is something I won't ever deny

They seem to be making sure
That I am able to see and accept
The things that are really going on in my heart
And the person I am trying to reject

Apparently they seem to understand
The inner turmoil I face everyday
They seem to want to make me more comfortable
Every time I feel certain ways

Apparently we have bonded
In a special and unexpected way
They are willing to do what is needed
Regardless of what comes their way

It seems they won't give up on me
Regardless of the things I come to say
Apparently they understand and accept the fact
That it's the only way

Even when I am angry
They seem to act like I have the right to say
They don't seem to judge me
Implying that tomorrow's another day

Strangely supported

Love for me is difficult
It's hard when we collide
Love has me upset
I'm far from feeling fine

I'm confused and conflicted
Not quite sure what to feel
It has me feeling insecure
I'm not sure what is real

Love causes me great pain
It has me in a state of distress
I don't know how to deal with it
I need time and space to rest

I feel down and out
Not sure which way to go
I feel at a loss
With time moving very slow

Love makes me sad
For reasons I can't help but forget
Love isn't easy
But my 'voices' keep me in check

They seem to guide me
When I don't know how to react
My 'voices' keep me grounded
They seem to always have me back

It's strange to be supported
In the way that I am
They seem to encourage me
There seem to have a plan

It's a strange old journey
Travelling through madness, sorrow and grief
They seem to be here to support me
To give me that much needed relief

But time moves very slowly
It moves to its own beat
It has its own order
I am not able to change it or compete

I'm trapped in a situation
That I helped create
I caused the problem
I realised that fact too late

I'm left in the aftermath
Of my own anger and hate
Then being told hope is out there
Even with things in this state

I'm not sure of what's on the horizon
I'm not sure what will come my way
Things aren't always clear
But again they say tomorrow is another day

Unwanted support

I seem to have a group of special 'people'
Helping me through the difficulties in my life
They seem to encourage and support me
Wanting me to see that I am really liked

They have come with a message
That hope isn't only slight
Also to teach me some skills
To help me when I need to fight

They want me to be comfortable
With the way I feel inside
Also suggesting
From them I shouldn't run and hide

They want me to accept the person I am
Showing me what a guy like that is really worth
They seem to show me a lot of respect
And imply that it's only what I deserve

I don't know what to do
It's not something I can easily accept
To be honest I always turn away from them
It's something I can't help but reject

I'm in a state of confusion
Feeling conflicted by what they say
I'm unsure what to do
Wanting them to put a different message on display

Travelling In Terror

I am on a journey and being supported on the way
I am being guided and have helpful hands around me who have chosen
to stay
They keep on insisting that I am special at all parts of the day
Implying that my heart is good especially when I feel things in particular
ways

They won't give up on me regardless of the mistakes I have come to
make
They imply that they are with me and willing to do what it takes
They seem to sincere telling me of the distance I've come
While being supportive nurturing telling me of the person I am going to
become

It's not an easy journey and their message is difficult to digest
They are always consistent and at times allow me to rest
Confused and conflicted not always sure what to believe
They are educating me and making things easier to conceive

This journey is hard and I am not always sure what direction to go
All I can do is slow down because of what I see in store
Unsettled and being told facts that are not easy to accept
I would feel better if they would let me be and these implications they
would allow me to reject

It's a real struggle with difficulties at every turn
I don't know what to do and my future is my biggest concern
My journey is challenging with what I am being told to be true
It has me feeling anxious and conflicted with no option that is easy to choose

Why can't I stop trusting them?
I'm filling with terror with every step I take
But I can't reject them
I am inclined to accept them which can leave me to thinking that it all could be a big mistake

Almost Overwhelmed

Why are they so persistent?
Why won't they let things be?
Why do they keep implying these things to someone like me?

Why won't they leave it alone?
Why do they want me to hold on?
Why do they keep thinking that it's something that's easy and something that I want done?

Why won't they learn that it's something I want kept away?
Why won't they learn that this is a position in which I want to stay?

What can I do?
What can I say?
What will it take for all this to go away?

Please leave me be, it's a road I'm not willing to take
it's painful and almost overwhelming
I'm in a place where I'm comfortable and here is where I'd like to stay

Shown Affection

I see things that surprise me
I see things that I would not expect
I find them almost overwhelming
I find them difficult to accept

It's not anything bad
It's something people would love to see
But it makes me angry
I'm not comfortable with what's being directed at me

They are so persistent
They keep looking at me in that way
I find it difficult
They seem to enjoy putting these things on display

They seem to be determined
They won't give up or let these points rest
They only show me when I don't expect it
And it annoys me that I can't help but accept

I want them to leave me alone
I want them to leave and let me be
This is the way I want it
Why is this difficult for them to see?

Why do they like me so much?
What is it that I've meant to have done?
most of the time I don't see myself as that good
Regardless of the distance I've come

They keep on showing me how they feel about me
They seem to like me a lot
I don't know what to do with them
They should know it has me in a state of shock

I know it's not so bad
To be accepting of someone who like you in that way
But I find it difficult to be around them
I'm inclined to push them away

I know it's not the end of the world
But from that I'm just inclined to part
When I see them I get so angry
I feel it from deep within my heart

I don't know how to change my feelings
It's something that is just part of me
I know they would like me to be more accepting
I've tried and it's just my pain is all I see

Attraction

They won't let me stop being attraction to women
They won't let that part of me die
They want me to keep feeling it
Like they know the truth about how I feel inside

They won't let me do what I want
They won't let me choose what I want my emotions to be
They keep proving me wrong
They challenge me and get me to consider and agree

I must really have a strong liking for women
It seems to be something they don't want me to destroy
They keep it alive regardless of how much it hurts
Or how much it comes to annoy

It's a cycle I have in my life
They keep highlighting things so that I see
I am really attracted to women
Even though when I feel how much I find it difficult to breathe

Whenever I feel this connection
My heart feels something I can't really describe
But there's pain attached to it
But on some level I like how it makes me feel inside

That's why I want it kept away from me
That pain is just too much to bear inside
It shouldn't be that every time I feel something for a female
It hurts which makes me want to run away and hide

What am I suppose to do with these circumstances that I have described?

What would anybody else to if this was how they felt inside?

How would they come to manage?

How would they get by?

What would they hope for?

What would they use as fuel to comply?

Beauty

Why do they keep showing me amazing beauty?
Why do they keep putting it on display?
Why won't they leave me alone?
Why won't they keep it away?

Why don't they understand that it's something that I want kept away
from me?
Why don't they understand that it's something I don't want to see?
Why can't they appreciate that it hard to be around?
Why can't they understand that it makes me feel down?

It can really upset me
Seeing things of such design
Why can't they understand without it I will do just fine?

I know how I should respond to it
But I don't function like how other people do
Seeing such things hurts me
And makes me feel angry and blue

Why won't they leave me alone?
What's so special about someone like me?
What have I done to deserve this?
I wonder what the answer could be.

Confusion Part 2

Have you ever been so confused you didn't know where to turn?
Did you wonder what to do and what was left for you to learn?

Have you ever felt conflicted because of what you saw in store?
Was it hard to get used to because you felt things you have never felt before?

Have you ever been full of fear because you didn't know how to react?
Have you ever been so sensitive to things and didn't know how to act?

Have you ever wondered how other people make it through such trials?
Have you ever wondered how they seem to know what to do even if only for a while?

Have you ever felt things that you didn't know how to define?
Have you ever had your perception of things change regardless of how you were inclined?

Have you ever wanted it all to be over because it messed with your mind?
Have you ever seen things that make it hard to unwind?

Have you ever faced things in a way that amplified the pain?
Have you ever been driven to exhaustion because of the stress and pain?

Have you ever wondered why it came into your life?
Have you ever wondered why things only seemed to be alright?

I wish I knew what to do with the way that I feel
I wish I knew what direction to go because some parts of my life are
losing its appeal

Considerate

None of my emotions are wasted
They won't pass them by
They keep responding to them
Wanting me to feel ease inside

They try to be gentle
Trying to soothe my pain
They be really careful
Wanting peace that I gain

They seem to be caring and considerate
Trying to give me much needed relief
They seem to keep it simple
Wanting me to stand comfortably on my feet

It's like they know my emotions get difficult
When I look upon certain things
But they don't hide this fact from me
They try to heal me from within

They are very consistent
Always showing me things when I don't expect
It's as if they want me to respond to it
Like they know it's something I would never really reject

To me they are taking a risk
It could take a turn for the worst
I can't hide from my feeling from them
The discomfort must be something I deserve

I find it really difficult
But they seem to be keeping the pace
I don't know what to do with what I see
But it seems like only a little taste

Appreciated

I have a unique element that has entered my life and they have come to support me and reinforce within me that things can one day be alright

They are like my family who have all come together to help and they are very accepting and love me when I am unable to do so myself

They like to remind me that love is something I deserve in my life and they like to encourage and reassure me when I think for me it's not right

My thoughts, hopes, opinions and dreams these are very important to them as well as my experiences and the things I have seen

They understand the difficulties I face because of the things I have said and done and they don't want me to underestimate what I am capable of or the distance I have come

There is a constant message they repeat because they want it to be made clear
"Hey you, you're loved and to us you are held as dear"

Tolerance

I'm not allowed to hate
I can't feel that way
I'm not allowed to do it
Any part of the day

I have to be understanding
I have to accept of what people display
I have to care that people only behave the way they do
Because they don't know any other way

I can't be judgemental
I have to respect what people have to say
I have to be helpful
Hopeful for people to find their way

I have to be patient
Letting people live life and be
Being there to give advice
Hoping they will accept that from me

This is the way
I'm being guided to be
I have to be strong
Even though some things are difficult to see

Hope

Do you know what it's like to wonder and not being able to find
with everybody telling you that things will be fine?

It's frustrating to think or even to hear
Hearing such words are difficult when hope is not near.

Do you know what it's like when fear is all inside
they are telling you such things that are filled with lie?

It's horrible to think or even be on such a journey
with things being hard and you're only making it nearly

The best things to do when a time are like this
is to sit back and resist while enjoying the simple things.

Times like this don't last forever
by holding on you'll gain strength in every endeavour

Slowly but surely it will start to pick up speed
finding around you everything you need

Hope will begin to grow and calmly you'll see
these things can change in ways you wouldn't believe

Guided by the wind

The wind seems to guide me
The wind seems to know the truth
The wind get's in the way when I don't know what to do

I try to go on instinct
Trying to the right thing
The wind get's in the way and behaves like he's my kin

He helps me to think
When I'm doing something I'm not supposed to do
Helping me when I'm lost and I don't have a clue

It's intention is to help correct my behaviour
So that I do the best that I can
He seems to do it according to a greater yet simple plan

He's Like my guardian
Who is willing to argue with me and fight
Insisting that I be sincere and always do that is right

Loved by the wind

The wind seems to love me, he seems to want to make it known and it gets in the way when the painful feelings start to grow

He seems to be there when I'm in a state of despair and the way he interacts with me is like he really cares

He's never there when I want, he comes when it's right and he comes at the time when I need support to put up a fight

He can be very sincere, it's not just hugs all the way and he tells me what I need for those painful feelings to go away

It's not always fun some feeling have to stay,
It's not always fun some feelings have to be faced another day

I'm glad he's my friend it's interesting to see him from day to day and I'm really glad to know him and to know that he loves in Allah the All Mighty's way

Trees

The trees seem to be able to sense me
They seem to know what it is I am feeling
The trees seem to be telling me things that I can't help but find appealing

They seem to know my pain
They seem to know the difficulties I face
They seem to know all this and want to help get me out of this state

They seem to really understand me
They seems to be telling me things to help give me hope
They seems to know that at times I find it hard to cope

I find them very supportive
I find relevance in what they express
I find they are knowledgeable they seem to know about success

They seem to really like me
But only when I hold on to truth
They seem to encourage me and remind me of the things I could lose

I'm in a state of wonder
Could this really be true?
Would trees support me when I am in need, feeling sad or simply don't
know what to do?

Jihad

Struggling and striving is all well and good
Without being patient and understand
It get's misunderstood

This takes practice
There is a discipline at play
You should try doing it each and everyday

If you need help
Get people involved
This can help while you're waiting for yourself to evolve

It depends on you intention and how able you are
When you'll get it right
It's the kind that will help you with your problems even if they are only slight

The goal that you want should also be right
You should be determined and willing to defend and fight
Concentrate on the positives even if they only seem slight

Even though it is hard it is worth it in the end
Then things will get better
Then you'll be able to contend

New beginnings

They have given me a confidence boost
They have made me more comfortable and bought my
life more ease
Life can still have its difficulties
I suppose for now that's the way it's meant to be

It can be hard moving forward
The pain is still real
Thankfully now it has variations
I can notice differences in the way things feel

I am becoming better and more consistent
Finding new ways to hold on to hope
These new skills helps
I've gained strength when climbing that slippery slope

At times it can still be difficult
It can be hard for me to relate
I'm still finding difficulties when love and affection
But find myself more comfortable when feeling that way

I'm going to keep striving forward
Holding on to what I know is true
Trying to picture the man I could one day become
Having that Impacts what I do

It's not very easy
With the memories of the things that I have done
The good thing is I have good friends
Telling me of the distance I have come
I hold on as tight as I can
To the new memories that they're gave
Trying to consider
How much stronger I've been made

When I look at relationships
With all the positive aspects that the entail
I find myself thinking of what it could be like for me
Holding on to the fact of it becoming real

My journeys still ongoing
I have a lot more skills I need to learn
Now seeing it possible to gain that connection
That I like everyone else deserves

I want to keep moving forward
Using what I'm being taught to be true
Love will come around
So try to be happy, not sad, misty eyed and blue

The Simpsons

The Simpson's seem to respond to me, and they behave like they know that I'm there and the Simpson's seem to acknowledge me when I am in a state of despair

They are quick to tell me what they feel about the decisions I have come to make, especially about me and relationships like where I stand is a big mistake

They seem to understand the things that I find difficult and try and help elevate that pain, Marge Simpson even tried to console me and guide me to a better decision that should be made

I'm not ready for that, is what I told her, it's really difficult, is the point that I made, she tried to push the fact that I have to face it, but I told her to leave and then she got upset and went away.

Joy

Life can make you wonder and fill you up with joy
 just like a baby playing with their first toy

What a beautiful thing to be in a state without having any worries
they play with toys and find it really funny

With a bright possible future and their life could become really grand
which depends on what they learn whilst they grow and where they
choose to make their stand

Additional poems about someone special to me. someone who gave me a chance and I feel I must share

The one I loved

You should know I loved you
You were more than just a friend
You were the person with which
I wanted to be with till the end

You gave me comfort
You bought me a lot of joy
You showed me love
The type I didn't want destroyed

You are very special
Someone who is hard to find
I thought my search was over
But I guess you weren't meant to be mine

I miss you so much
You were what were missing from my life
You were what I needed
Hope was re-entering my sight

Now that it's over
With our relationship coming to an end
I would have liked to be able to see you
I would have liked to be your friend

I wanted to be there to support you
I wanted to be someone one which you could depend
I wanted to be someone you could lean on
I wanted to be your special friend

I would have liked to be around you
So around you would be another who cared
But I suppose you don't need me
I understand
This I just had to share

Memories

My time with you was special
I will never forget
You gave me a chance
Me you did accept

The way you talked to me
Helped me to feel
Nice sensations
And things I wanted to be real

The look in your eye
Always bought about a smile
The way it made me feel
I hadn't felt for a while

I will fondly remember
That time we spent as one
It will help me on my journey
With me thinking of the distance I've come

My only hope
To find someone like you
I wonder if it's even possible
That fact impacts all that I do

I have to be patient
If I want to find someone like you again
But I don't know if that is even possible
At times I feel like I must settle and pretend

To a special women

How did she behave with me?
How much of me did she accept?
When I was with her I received kindness and always got her respect

She was very nurturing
Always said things that struck a special cord
She always surprised me and the effect was that I felt reassured

She is a unique lady
Someone I thought was a distant dream
I felt really secure
I felt like I was part of a team

She was very affectionate
Because of her I came to be able to see
What it was like to be loved
And what I wanted it to be

What I came to experience
I will never come to forget
She will always be someone special to me
The fact that it ended was my main regret

To someone special

To my dearest Friend
You helped me to see
There were choices and options available for someone like me

You gave me strength
You bought me joy
You made me feel loved like I was a very special boy

I was given hope
I was loved and accepted
You were always warm
And I was always respected

You were honest and firm
And true to your word
You gave me something
I didn't think I deserved

You showed me kindness
And helped me believe
That changed was possible
For someone like me

I experienced comfort
More calming than I thought I could expect
You have a special place in my heart
And that I will always protect

I hoped to give you something
That everybody needs
I hoped to give you some support
And to your life bring some ease

I want you to know
You are very dear to me
And its only your happiness
I am wanting to see

One thing I'll tell you
If it was ever going to come true
I think I could have said
I LOVE YOU
To someone like you

Confession

Dear friend
I miss having you in my life
Your were a good reason
for me to begin putting up a fight

You'd given me strength
You got me to hold on
You gave me hope
You helped me to be strong

There's not many people
with whom I feel I can share
When I think of you
I know you were someone who cared

I miss seeing you
I liked it when you were around
Even the silence
You made it a peaceful sound

You bought my heart ease
And provided a safe space
you gave me something
That's going to be difficult to replace

I don't want to complicate you life
I would just like you to know
You will always be wanted
but I know I have to let go

Please don't be mad with me
On me you've just made an impression
You've exposed me to something
You taught me some valuable lessons

Again I know it's a little much
And even if you don't agree
Just writing this helped me
In ways people only dream

I just had to tell you
What our relationship meant to me
You are someone special
I enjoyed being part of your team

My special friend

It was nice to have someone bring some warmth to my life
She made me feel warm
I had hope in my sight

It was the kind of experience one doesn't easily forget
I felt like I had achieved something
I felt like I had success

She was someone special
Someone who is hard to find
She was reassuring
At times she was extremely kind

Now that it's over and it has come to an end
I feel at a loss
I have lost my special friend

One thing I've learnt and it goes like this,
Love is important
And yours I will always miss

Difficult lesson learned

I destroyed something that had bought hope to my life
Things were changing and my future was looking bright

I had something special and was hoping to experience more
It had me excited about my future and what could have been in store

I was gaining strength, comfort and confidence was re-entering my heart
I felt wanted and needed and from her I didn't want to part

My view on life was changing and I was becoming able to believe
My life could improve and that was something I really wanted to see

I was gaining something of value, something which is very rare
My surroundings were changing I was leaving the area of despair

Time was moving slow and every moment I will miss
I enjoyed spending time with her even the silences are moments to
reminisce

It was something I needed something I can't ever forget
Those memories are precious, something I will always protect

I wish I hadn't of destroyed one of the most special parts of my life
But what can I do? It happened our relationship must not have been
right

I am still hopeful of what my future could be
I am going to try to be patient to see what The Most Merciful would provide for me

I ask only of Him and hope He would allow beauty to re-enter my life
And hopefully I will take better care of it so I can experience what happiness for me is meant is to be like

Printed in the United States
By Bookmasters